Mysterious Lockdown

Fatal humanity

Part 1

TABLE OF CONTENTS

TABLE OF CONTENTS

CORONA

After a hundred years, an epidemic exposes as a demon for everyone social media is only a source of knowledge as all are at home, which fresh brain. I am also a part of the usual people. Loose time is prompting me to write something. Time supports for exploring an innovative story. Yet writing is my diet, fingers spread. Where T.V is enjoying people writing escalates my mind. T.V is continually exploring the epidemic role in society. Government addresses' JANTA LOCKDOWN' for securing people. Government chooses the first day on SUNDAY. People hold the rules of government seriously. But the next day on Monday people subdues the law by showing avoidance of power. Unstoppable announces of government for securing are exposing responsibility of government. Police are marching in each street, in each corner and in the Chowk. The whole world belligerence is struggling against the epidemic CORONOVIRUS. States are also focusing on the eradication of the pandemic. After LOCKDOWN people are not taking seriously, then the government takes steps for CURFEW. Despite CURFEW people rush, even regular announcements alert all. The government functions are running well but although there is a picture of inhumanity. In Italy, people are dying on the road even authorities do not dare to cure them. Powerful countries seem helpless. Even in America at Newyork 50,000 people captivate in the paw of a pandemic. But in the presence of Prime Minister Narender Damodar Dass Modi Ji India keeps easily control on this demon. Prime Minister says

"Try to understand the seriousness of this pandemic. The priority of life is salvation. Outside of our home is death. Yamraj is on the roads in the veil of coronavirus. It is essential to Safe yourself and your family."

A small exuberance by Prime Minister of India to safe a country like a Sungrebe of central and South America bird. America today has lost about 50,000 people due to Coronavirus, is a global superpower of the earth. World's first nuclear weapon develop the country which also used it's in the Second World War. American President Trump says," There is no need to lock down America. The economy is more imperative than lockdown country." If I am not wrong my thoughts trying to ahead in the right direction, the Indian Prime Minister sure on Healthy then happy economy. American President makes an effort on securing the economy than health. Two persons have varied psychology on the same topic. Two psychologies crash in the same situation, one is focusing on health and other on the economy. We can say money-minded cynosures are throwing the citizens in the circuit of burning. Whereas heartfelt and systematic personalities strive to magnetism in the host of unity, I think it has rightly said," If there is rain, then there is greenery." When people watch and listen to this news on T.V just one word in response America must consider. Trump must lend an ear to the public who have given a chance to governance on America. I think the cold air will invaluable in the winter season same as sun rays in the summer. In childhood children, meaningless action exhale melody of happiness while the same deed in adulthood causes him/her a ridiculous subject. President Trump is a responsible personality. I expect he will inevitably command sharp paces.

I am scanning with my eyes whether I am at home but can feel to listen through people. Some displays keep examining directly with my optic. On the time of LOCKDOWN, I am taking rest till late morning. Habitually, I got up at 4'o' clock. But from twentieth March I felt entirely free. Why I do not know while I have a lot of work perhaps I was thinking life stop now. Just one day before I was on leave but that time I did not know that I had to live at home for a long time, but It is correct. Just one day before LOCKDOWN I was preparing my document for a new job, for this, I need to go to another school for attesting documents. First of all, I went to senior secondary school from where I got my Matriculation certificate, met with the old-time memories. As soon as I entered the school, I asked the peon," Is Principal Mam inside?"

Peon: Yes.

My feet without stopping entered inside the office as a classical dancer dances without distraction, she was discussing something with her colleagues. I stood by the chair and asked Namaste.

She responded thoughtfully: Namaste.

I took my seat without permission because both were busy in the discussion.

As soon as I returned to a comfortable position, she asked me," How are you?"

I: Quite well. And you?

Principal: She lost her brightness.

I: I had a purse and two bags while her brain captivated to settle things. Then she suddenly flipped up her eyes and observed me regularly. Hurriedly, I supplicated her I need your a little help.

Principal: Sure. Do you know we visited at your school last week?

I: Nothing brothers. Please attest my document.

As soon as I said to her," She pointed me out for the next room where a clerk was working. Quickly, outwardly stating any work stood up and entered another room. There was not a clerk but a computer operator here. The computer operator was a female who was busy on the phone with someone else. Room employed with disorganised series of account books by the clerk because exam days were operating by the authority, everyone was intrusive. I asked her," Where is the clerk?

Computer operator responded: He has gone. Maybe he will not come. R is another female helper accountant she can do. As I receive the name of R, my cerebrum lost in the past's beat.

Poison

But I ignored her reference because I do not want to meet her. She was a foe of her family, who had silently hit to her psyche without knowing her. She intended to obtain only money for fulfilling desires.

Whether right or wrong means for assembling money she did. She had played a willy hoax to abducting her sister for a calculating boy. S is a boy who belongs to a Muslim family whose mother is a partial lady. A greedy family who wants to get dowry from a daughter-in-law, But she belonged to a Sikh family. Her family is living on rent home but more educated in relationships. Their Daughter has married a Muslim boy without the presence of parents. Though her parents embraced her, their son-in-law supplied a poisonous dose speeches whenever he captured on the opportunity. Rati's life is as an idiom which tends to confuse that unfamiliar with them. Her sister always derived her motivation. Everything will be perfect if you spill the beans. But Rati always says," Once a bird flies never returns." Rati has laid down arms before his on limited speech. He does not bother any. Problematic and forcefully complaint is a tool to keep him separate from others. Rati's sister has assisted in the hospital on the birth time of her daughter. Just before the birth Of her daughter, she endeavours to speak with her. Both sisters were duplicate for each other in appearance.

As time passed, the poison of common krait started work on her sister. Rati's brain was under the control of the common krait. A group of common krait was a symbol of poison. A crowd of common krait lived in the Saraswati place. The second house and the second mother of the children is the bowl of poison. On the return of jealous, their group's one female played a long-run game. Rati's beauty was uncomparable to nature's beauty. Her hair complexion, large black eyes, sunning forehead, bellow smile including young skin lured others. Rainbows all colours reflect in her grace. That is why a group of venom was assembling the bowl of poison in the heart. Their inner soul was swallowing Rati's future like Napantheses. The first assault was on through her marriage on the family.

The first woman asked," Why do you not married?"

Rati: We are planning to buy a home as our home is on rent.

The first woman: Why will you contribute to buying the home? You should focus on yourself. Are you waiting for wrinkles?

Rati: No, you are contemplating wrong? Late marriages are acceptable in society. We all are unmarried. Support to one another is the power of our siblings.

The first woman: Really, you are foolish. Why does your sister not investing herself earning?

Rati: She is running home's regular essentials. She can take aid from both.

The first woman: Why does she not study ahead? Dear innocent subsequent she has prepared a life's route.

Rati: What do you mean?

The second woman: The palm fell on the sky. She will exist on this earth on your efforts.

Rati: You mean, she will not work.

The second women: Yes, dear.

We have a boy who is an accountant. He is the only son in the house who runs home like you. He is a responsible guy like you. He has his own house. He has a father, mother and a married sister and can do all households. You will live like a queen and have not a burden of economic responsibility. You will not have freight of giving rent and the bill of ration. You have your own home. After in-laws, that home will be yours also deliver the order of her volition. We will talk with you tomorrow.

Rati: No, Firstly, I will discuss in my home. If my parents say, "yes", then I will converse with him.

Rati returns house from school daily routine. Summer afternoon scorches her body so that the mother prepares homemade lemon water. Rati chats with drinking drink, her delights reflect on the face. She can read her face and heart. The mother responses she will consult with her father.

Rati: Ok, mam.

Sleeping her diet, she goes for a deep sleep inside where she lives with her sister. Both are opposite. While Rati is an extrovert, her sister is introvert. Her sister feels boredom very soon while Rati does everything in depth. But both have something same. The response of stimulation of good or bad can catch. Both are holy because of the spiritual atmosphere of the home. Both sisters have self-actualisation of divine powers. Their religious devotion reflects in the bare-footed resolution is troublesome. They get up at 4'o' clock and have a bath. They wear almost the same colour clothes on a religious journey. They start their pious quest bare-footed about fifteen kilometres at 5 'o'clock. They return from the temple with an innovative attachment at 9 'o'clock in the holidays. Then they with mother chant in front of Maa Durga. They keep fast on Durga festival. On Durga festival, they cook special meals with potatoes, Sabudana khichdi, Sabudana vada, Banana Payasam(kheer), Sabudana kheer, Jeera Potato(aloo poshto), fruit chaat with Imli, Khaskhas with dry fruits. Their neighbours also wait for tasting meals. Whereas Rati is a playful girl, her sister is a simple living girl. Rati believes in God Krishan thoughts while her sister shows devotion in the role of Rama. But therefore, both follow the rule of Dharm and keep stand on the opposition of Adharm. Both keep continuing her hard work against struggling life. Her sister has time for sleeping only two hours. Her day and night are identical images of striving. White colour reflects in the black hole of her eyes. It seems her head always down for bowing on white tone. Her eyes and body have forgotten the softness of gist. Stubborn day and night have disappeared the beauty of nature and family. And so her robotic essence has bound. Rati's wishes are a compact for charm products. She has a love for elegance. God-gifted inadequacy dare not to stop her choices. Rati furnishes the tips of beauty to sister for all time grace. Her affectionate fingers spread for sparkling the others' covering and unbound tender layer of footings is the cherish guru of the Natraj's dance steps. Rati's tentacles taste of running wheels of needles. Books run with the music of movies. Her cognition is a treasure for family and slaps oncoming difficulties. Rati's claws have the strength to move the handle of wheels. Making delicious food is her hobby, but a great time for others. Rati is Navratan of family. Both sisters' choices are different. Rati's interest in music, dance, cooking, beauty resources, stitching, dish washes, watching movies and shopping is gest of her life. Rati only avoids to cleaning home and kneading flour. She always says," My finger's joint will puff in the full youth. So I do not like."

Rati always says," Smile is the best tool to beat the world. People can betray just through a smirk whether you want or not." On the other hand, her sister loves to karma. She believes in Karma is Dharma. Her sister is also like music, classical dance. She wants to acquire a higher position and respect in the education sector for breaking the chain of inadequacy. Her sister dreams of marrying a more precious fame celebrity. Her sister character name I always say," Keep on keeping on! Go the distance. It isn't over until you win. However, you want to word it you keep moving the direction of your goal! Goals may take a long time, weeks, months, years. Don't stop. Don't setback, no matter how trivial or how difficult, check you!

If you find a crevice in your way, build a bridge or climb down & back out. You might not make ahead promotion during the time you are surmounting your obstacles, but you are still moving towards the goal. Always have pertinacity, never give up!!"

Her sister is a lamp of the home. She has won the trust of her family. The economic trajectory of her home shows that the independency of the family on her. She spends the whole life in the black ink words. Her birth, young age and running near old age hark to the sounds of family members, dropping pens on the ground, changing the side of the paper on the end of space like a baby and the silence face of walls with the tranquil brain. Her big black peepers awake twenty- two hours out of twenty-four hours. Seldom she forgets to feed herself. All the days and nights earns the same cent of tiredness. A single penny means a life-breath from lungs Rati leaves the ashes from burn heart to see her long hair and big eyes on the face. A thin-layered body speaks the perpetual running brain footed expedition. Her responsible journey never allows stopping on the rim of the topsy-turvy circumstance. Her inner faith in herself gives a strength ahead. She determines never leave a weakness of necessities which she has faced in the absence of the father. Father's cost is invaluable before gems. Often she misses the urgency of a father. Disregarding her father has run from home at the age of ten so that he does not have the value of family. Her mother, who also belongs to zero level poverty were two hands earning looks hand-to-mouth, has believed in education. The absence of literacy interests her in the world of books. Her mother picks a choice from the past hardships. Her mother never regrets three children, especially for two girls. Often she says in the group of women," Girls are the mirror of society, especially for men. I have three sons who will light in the dark of scarcity. I will not abject for girls while the boy's mother will have. My daughters are my sons who break the chain of the rich cerebrum. Their vibrant brain will surprise the vertebra in the field of boy's sector. Their eternal presence will create an epitome before other girls. My inner soul never distinguishes between them. Girls are the soul of the home then how a body runs without a soul. Girl's womb is a breath of the earth."

But she did not know in the future lap. When speaks with them her face sparkles with the vast confidence, even her neighbour woman tries to steer out following time. The time displays the rising sun and setting sun outside of the home. Among these women, her owner woman also occupies a place. She just notices her belief between daughters. Her owner's head is cooking a blueprint to demean her in the group. Her rancid mind is roasting into ashes. When she lost her patience of praising daughters, she stops her by saying," Hun, Girls should not more supply of freedom, after all, she will cook food in the kitchen. You are more expecting from girls. You should focus on her son because he will feed you. Girls have to go after marriage. How can you keep them the whole life? Girls should settle first at a young age. Girls are the perfume of roses who spreads fragrance from one home to others. Do not think higher stay feet on the earth. Keeping confidence on future Rati's mother says," Look Raj sister she has admitted her elder daughter in M.A English in college. And see yourself you have blocked her daughters way after plus two. You should receive from her. I will send my daughters to college for further study. Girls should look like a human being later the problem will not create in the community. Why do men society glance at girls like a girl? Whether a man or woman must see a human. " A silence comes and place on a seat among women. Suddenly the owner of the home call returns in mind a sweater of a married daughter remain for knitting. The owner of home alarms with the sound of words O! mother of Rati stop this debate on girls let us knit the sweater of my daughter. Rati's mother replied with an attitude of ignoring this is lunchtime. My children are coming from school. So I am going for cooking food for them. Tomorrow will retrieve me. Anguish heart calls her and refuses to knit the sweater of a conservative woman. Her eyes lament for the scarcity of money. Her every step ahead towards daughters hope for the rainbow. Mother's ascertainment is growing to children firmness for climbing a high mountain of appetites. After the setting of the sun, a dull speck encompasses the entire universe, the repetitions of the black blabber encroaching her eardrums. Her eyes open in the virgin fog.

Shots of altercation

Next day afternoon decorates with taunts of efforts to separate sisters. Nowadays, a group of women in fragrance noon discuss the pros and cons of others' children. Unaware Rati's mother goes in the group for diverting the thoughts a sudden attack of complaints rinse the brain and heart. Neighbour ego is trying to show the path of etiquettes.

Neighbour: Your elder daughter must respect elders.

Rati's mother: Why? What did she do now?

Neighbour: On the returning from the school, she never cares who sits on the roads. She bends her head and passes from us. Her face shows the neglection to us. After all, we are neighbour she should talk with us.

Rati's mother: She does not have time. Is she only my daughter? Is she not your daughter? My daughter wakes up early 4 'o clock and returns at evening 5'o clock. You should concede her condition of physique and mind. The dusk of the day lost conscious stamina. My daughter better knows to treat elders. Her furious expression chides them and infuriated body language signal to return home. In the evening Rati's daughter is coming along on the road, women group's chatting continuously, while she crosses near the women a neighbour calls her for accusing to speak with them. I Rati's sister has not the capacity to stay there although she stays with a blow.

I: Namaste to all aunties. How are all of you?

Neighbour: It's ok, today how you remember calling wish to us.

I: You call me so that I wish you.

Neighbour: O! You do not want to communicate with us.

I: No, It's not mean.

Neighbour: Whatever you mean, we are giving you a suggestion.

I: Yes. Move head with wide eyes expresses confidence with ego.

Neighbour: When you cross this road you should move with evening wish to us.

I: But why?

Neighbour: O! Perhaps you do not know.

I: What?

Neighbour: We are editors who must have every news.

I: You means the printing press is running daily gossip.

Neighbour: Yes, You must enrol here then go ahead.

I: Oh! Ask what do you want to inquire?

Neighbour: What do you earn nowadays?

I: Hmmm! The extremely crafty question, I think for the artful query must have the sly response. She smiles with large eyes and to flout nose says whatever all get the same mine.

Neighbour: Still, how much? Have you applied for a government job?

I: Government job mmmm. Where is the government job nowadays? You know the government is already naked henceforth how can you think about the government job.

Neighbour: You do not tell the right way to reply. With a laugh contemplating I will invent your all secret one day, you cannot hide from me more days.

I: She is thinking, how can I save myself from a ghost?

Other women snapping the fingers, call her and jeer her she will not leave you. A sound of chuckling on the road is giving the signal of stoppage. Other women ask her to go home rest of information give her the next day.

Neighbour: Do you have an account in the bank?

I: yes.

Neighbour: How much saving do you have?

Rati's sister feels strange and discussing how stupid aunty does question. Finally, she moves toward the neighbour and puts a query.

I: Well, aunty I have overheard you have one crore in your account.

Other women attack, ha! You do not tell us. Quite sharp, the tone of the jeering moves toward neighbour aunty! In the crowding of voice Rati's sister turns to home. She arrives home and tells the story of checking on the police block.

Mother: Police block?

I: Wahi! Press reporter with investigators neighbour.

Mother and daughters laugh and spread the flower fragrance in the small room. Time passed, subsequent a week, Rati expresses a desire for marriage. A mother discusses with father although he tries to ignore, mother imposes on him for trying. Mother settles to call teachers for a meeting. Rati's happiness has no limit she does as her mother says. Following day, both teachers come or give detail in limited words. They do not open the original story of the boy's family. All simply retain a line boy is a library of literacy. Your daughter will joy there. You should focus on a boy. Leave all the boy is the library of literacy. Your daughter will joy there.

They impose at any rate while her parents are feeling something wrong.

Parents: We want to go to the boy's home.

Teachers: Sure, fix time.

Parents: Whenever you and the boy like, we have not any objection, send a message.

Teachers: Following fifteen days, teachers blame, your parents said they would fix.

Rati: No, you said.

Teachers: They see each other why do we need to lie? Your parents do not want to marry. You should take a step for marrying. We will meet you at a boy if you are ready.

Rati: No, outwardly parent permission I cannot take a step.

Teachers: Are you a child? You should take decisions yourself. Today we will call him in the recess, and you will communicate with each other. Nothing will happen, and we are with you.

Rati: No, I will not.

Teachers: Yes, you will.

Teachers are an epitome of Gurus though here a life of an innocent girl is going towards the death bed in disguise manner. Lectures are formality in the recent era. Teachers are bound in their intricacies. Or somewhere the venom of vengeance is employed in the separation of relationships. School boundaries where a character is a base of life, there is a plan to demolish an innocent girl. A bell of recess rings they turn toward the lab. They contact a boy and says her to chat with him.

Boy: Hi! My name is S.

Rati: Hi! My name is Rati.

Boy: Are you free?

Rati: No, recess time.

Boy: Have you take lunch?

Rati: No, I will take in the sixth period.

Boy: I send biodata, Did your parents see?

Rati: Yes.

Boy: What are their reaction?

Rati: Silent.

Boy: Ok, can we meet tomorrow?

Rati: No.

Colleagues are saying her says yes. Rati is comprehending their gestures although she shows as she does not know. She passes the phone to her colleagues. They insist on her still she does not. Rati returns home tells her mother. Mother refuses to talk again.

Mother: Your colleagues will leave you alone. We will go home then take the next step. You are mature. I hope you know, What is the meaning of hard work for us. Hard work is our wealth and respect. Inadequacy is not so bad while discourtesy is the death for us. Always remember stand alone like a tree if a human attitude for a reason. Consequently, fix meeting with us.

Her desire for marriage is reflecting on her face beside a liability of esteem is standing her layout.

Rati: Ok.

Next day she goes to the school with a bunch of excitement to school, she gathers them and asks them," My parents require to meet, inform me when they will appear."

Teacher: We will ask them.

Rati: No, Ask know fix today.

Teachers even now are playing a game. Shrewd women are ready for barking like street dogs. They are chameleons who always willing to capture prey located some distance away. Corresponding teachers prey her for satisfying their ego avenge. Their avenge is masking with the welfare state. Their eyes converse with each other besides captivating to innocent hearts. They call to boy for fixing meet. He replies for meeting at five-thirty in the evening. They answer her of coming time of happiness. Today Rati's face glowing for thinking the coming love. She loves singing and sings a lovely song in her heart.

"We meet in the heart love,

We meet in the heart love,

listen to our feelings in the dive of aesthetic sense

We meet in the heart love

Mmmm Aaaaa Mmmm Aaaa Mmmm."

Her bliss of joy hypothetically high where a love floats in a special love. She arrives at home and transfers their message to parents. They will meet on Sunday at five-thirty. Mom, please on time! Father can disturb the schedule he does not time value. She is under stress on behalf of a father Who has an unimaginable purpose. The whole family focuses on him to success plan. On Sunday out of five members, four are waiting for the evening time and consequences. Rati phones to teachers at five ' o clock ask for going towards a new life. They respond sharply," We are already waiting from both sides response. A boy is on duty even now. He will free at six 'o clock. We will go at six clocks."

Rati: She conveys the message to parents.

Her father is as a being hyper. Her father's hypertension is contracting the heart of family members. She again telephones them, that extent they miss the call. She phones them about ten to fifteen times although they receive after one hour. Rati feels ashamed before family. After one hour they disclose a crafty an idea and say send their parents our home. A dirty base of a pizza who prepares a horrible love story where her parents are going insulting her parents after arriving. When parents visit, she does not come outdoor. About fifteen minutes they spend outward of their home. She is a characterless woman who earns money the corrupt way. She knows how to move men. A sly woman dances men on her gestures. She is busy on the phone, does not bother them. Fifteen minutes are a lesson of life how an idle man does not get respect from family as well as society. A narrow street of thoughts will assault they do not conscious contrast they are planning. When she leaves the addiction of phone, she invites them inside also giving a seat. They use a chair then she moves toward her neighbour's home, the second poison position. An avenger abode who is a second wife, a heart's hole child is an epitome of worse. A game planner of an innocent girl is playing cards. Teachers' husband is absent, and they are disguising their delaying part from the plan. They are waiting in the one home, and they are projecting in another home. Thence Rati is weeping in the heart, and here her sister dooms in tension. That evening does not kill its blackness. The artful women know her father ca not perceive in the night so that they wait of black coal night. Cunning women will commence airing on the road at seven-thirty.

A detriment of unawareness

Who knows that the cost of ignorance will remain in a memoir. A biography of Rati in which she will hang in a dreamy marriage is writing in the heart with a memoir pen. Parents who are ignorant of losing self-existence in society. Teachers inside home appear them a dark from there they cannot survive. Teachers' husband has returned as fix time at seven-thirty. As they turn, they show that they were hectic in daily routine. Middle teacher husband wishes her parents and says," Let's go we are so late." They stand up and go out of the home. Treasures husband and wife walk a talk inside about fifteen minutes till they are waiting. Her husband tells about a boy. A long six feet eleven-inch height, a little light from dark complexion, broad forehead covered with black hair, below the brow a pakora type nose with thick lips all are the introduction of the desired marriage boy. He has only four jeans with two shirts. He is also a little stress, lives in a Basti area and earns fifteen thousand per month. After ten minutes they come out after doorsteps they enter in their other artful's home. A dark piece of the night is now horrifying the spirit of parents when still they leave in the waiting road. Somehow they start the run for the reaching on the meeting point. Three middle people and Rati's parents are passing from the flat paths which seem unknown for father. Anyhow they arrive, yet throughout Rati's mother face look dull, and the heart fills with tension. The boy S is outside for waiting they meet him. The boy meets them though her parent's inner soul does not accept him. The credo is the internal response which draws a negative light towards him. The first look outside the home four to five stairs help raising the level from the road to the main gate. A narrow lane after ten steps an open courtyard gives the light of the sun. In the courtyards' left-hand other stairs are the way of coming life. A window of the kitchen is a fount of the fragrance of ingredients of the relishes. A foul of bathroom and aroma of flavourings render the panorama of the shrink of a young woman and inactivity. Even his mother has a facility of a servant, but an image of ignorance calls a necessity. Necessity does not prompt the reverence towards others. The boy's father's vender occupation mentions the level in society. And Rati's parents can easily guess the situation of the home. A forty years old bed yells the economic structure of the per member. They give chairs for sitting them and commence the inquiry of Rati's parents. An orthodox speculum is reflecting the predicted words which show the disgrace for Rati's parents.

Boy's father: Do you work?

Rati's father: No.

Boy's father: Why?

Rati's father: Business losses shatter the chain of courage.

Boy's father: Would you not keep start again?

Rati's father: Not now. I Will see in the future.

Boy's father: Might you have not money? How would you commence a business? Would you not trap in the job?

Rati's father: Wait, I will see where I will engage. We must focus on for what purpose we are here. My daughter is very innocent and soft. She is very talkative and keeps the desire to do a job. Still, she is doing a job. She is younger than two siblings. She does not go into the kitchen. Rati is very delicate moreover she will not carry the whole responsibility of home. How many members do you have in your home?

Boy's father: We are not many family members. Our daughter has married. We have not any objection to her job.

Teacher's husband: Its In-laws choice they want or not. Later marriage Parents' rights do not have possession of the daughter. Daughter spends life under in-laws decision.

Rati's father surprises listen to him, and he thinks what he is doing. He comes with us and favouring them. His inner heart apprehends the backstage performances which have settled down before. Unaware consciousness is now alarming after the little conversation. S boy invites them for seeing his room which he has built with a long time span. A bed and almirah seem he prove the picture of poverty and desire for marriage. Uncomplete tiles combine with cement is a public bathroom which shows the insecurity for a family. On the left side of the stairs, another public toilet has fixed the place furthermore unplastered walls tell the story of the separation of relations among them. That time Rati's parent have comprehended the economic background but not relations poison. They come down and request for leaving from here. They come outside the home with the S boy wishes them good-by. Both husbands of teachers crush the road with the dipper light whether Rati's father cannot perceive in the night. His bike expedition runs slow for ignoring the accidents. Somehow they hit the arrow on the target point of distance. Both husbands and wife turned into the home, and they do not bother about Rati's parents. However, Rati's parents ask them," Call me as your decisions will make." And they return home at 9'o' clock, there Rati and her sister are waiting with the craze. The racket of bike returns the answer to their questions. Their feet roll fast towards the gate and penetrate the bike with tired and desperate eyes. A tired parent defeat from before the love of a daughter but a lack of economic sector they are unable to marry her. They have a glass of water and express the perception of their role and the condition of the home. Parent asks her decision about a boy.

They say," There is a need for homemaker not a professional. Your desire works in the field how will you manage. That home and people demand a lot, hard worker daughter-in-law. There is a situation of below poverty line. You are so soft and have not filled this growth."

Daughter: I want to marry here. I like him, and everything will survive me. You do not take tension. I am mature, and I know what I am going to do. It's my life, and I have the right to live my breath."

Parent conceives the print of that family review. The inquiry of the family does not exhibit a valid average rate. Parents can perceive undoubtedly an invisible chain filled with forces of colours. It seems an adoption will give to the Pakistani army, which is very cruel, a highly disappointing delivery. Contemplative thoughts do not read the idea of the upcoming eras. On the opposite paw, daughter's meeting outside the home and school is burning the fire of assault young age. Now the chapter of the insulting family in each home has begun, and her behaviour about family changing. An injection of poison is ejaculating in the relationships. Subsequent the two months a call rings on his father's phone, he picks the call and speaks," Namaste uncle I am S boy from Basti. You did not answer, and we are waiting though you did not. Rati and I want to marry. We need nothing. I hope you will respond the next day."

Father: Teachers did not react to how I reply to you. I will see, ok.

Time is crossing fastly with the outside meetings of both in the return of hate towards Rati's family. Two months journey has stood the building in the backward of the issue. Rati's well-thinking brain has converted into hostility. The S boy believes in 'Tit for tat' whether a parent stands before him or another person. He just tries to remember her" She should take a look on loss or profit in relationships. Use the brain in contacts whether a close or far should utilise the focus on self profit. He has implanted venom of partition for elder siblings. A venomous revolution against family has decorated a platform of insult in the community. Consequent two months course decorates Heena on cards unaware of the progenitor.

Rati: Mom, today I am going to school for two hours give me breakfast first.

Mom: When will you return home?

Rati: Why?

Mom: Do you have misremembered today we will go to market.

Rati: I will return after two hours then.

Her sister I have discerned for the night newfangled. When she gets up at eight-thirty asks Is today not a government holiday.

Rati: Yes. I know though Principal calls. Also, What can I do?

Her sister: If today is a holiday head bath will wash after returning. Why are you in a hurry?

Rati is delightful for preplanned marriage with outsiders and Principal. She is relishing her beauty and dreams of newly wedding coming life. Her sister has a fear of doom and understood her future in tough situations. Her brain presses under stress and always tries to find a way of coming out this tide. Simply she evermore considers failing before opposition, and she can not speak about waves. Mother is in the kitchen preparing breakfast for son, and a son is in the bathroom, and the sister is on the bed, and her father is in the corridor. She goes out and starts her Activa as she moves, Rati recollects that she has misremembered her make- up kit. Rati drives back gear and holds eyes on the handbag. Her sister has no limit of astonishment when she picks it. Today her sister does not recognise the day as every day comes. This time mother frees from daily kitchen household. As Rati goes out, the mother follows her to the gate. Rati rambles some trolls on the ride and then she sees backwards to her mother for a while.

Mother asks," Have you remained anything?"

Rati: I do not want to go today.

Mother: Do not go, return my child. Send a message to school you can not come.

Rati: No, I have to go.

And she quits that road forever. Her thoughts awake from the dark past as she receives the sound of whispering of some one.

After ignoring R she returns to Principal office, as Principal seeing her on returning, she again lost her brightness. Because she had helped in the willy act or was in a dangerous corner, I do not focus on it.

I: Clerk is not in the office.

She: You can wait.

But she does not want to stay there then decides to return and accommodates her documents in the bag. When her eyes were seeing down, Principal gazed her regularly. Her face was pouring infinite love for her. I was unaware of this.

I: confidently say Thanks.

She (Principal)does not say any word. Her expressions are revealing her communication. Now the second journey of the other school starts. A school building which has seen almost two decades of city, speaking a story through the old students' approach and teachers' wrinkles of the skin, the utterances way of communication of weakening physiology on the changing time pace signifies the fluid form of the sky. The brother of I character has played in the dirt. The sound of tapping on the benches in childhood is also a magnifier of memories. I and M both characters go to school. He observes school very keenly and feels fantastic. Subsequent twenty years, his senses undergo a new cognisance, like a newborn child who comes out from the layers of darkness refreshing his eyes. His cognitive ability is funding the reminiscences. Good essence of peon comes out from the office and asks why do we come here?

M: I want to meet Principal sir.

Peon: Sure, but sir is not available now. You have to wait.

M: Ok. When will he come?

Peon: Maybe nine or nine-thirty, please sit here. You are not telling the reason for coming here.

M: I have some document to attest it.

Peon: Please wait.

I and M wait for Principal. M sits in the waiting room and his sister I wait outside the office. A person enters and requests to sit hereabouts. She is observing intensely to each wall and room. In the middle of the ground flower bed holds a smell of scents. A teacher is testing the robustness of learners by the operative paper of mechanical acquaintance. The culture is still alive by giving respect to touch the feet of the gurus. The relationships between students and gurus are like a guider, not a dominator. Brother M arrives out and calls his sister I. A large hall room in which a kitchen is available for staff members and guests on the left side of mine. In front of the Principal office sitting arrangement has done for all. On the right side of my stairs, which are dealing with the space for teachers who unroll the speciality of learning among students, a fully systematic classification, their usage of space displays the construction of creativity. I impressed to view it. In front of the Principal office on the right side clerical staff have passed, the material of office records in the almirah. In front of almirah, a computer and a chair proof a technical procedure, its documentation kept the workload stress on the employee. A pile of documents always horrify to the employee which overloads mentally as well as physical stress, remain a stressful and timeless schedule, In the entry of the clerical room a table and a chair place for the absent clerk but today Mr. Sharma has to arrive for attesting our document. The character name I am quite happy for attaining a serene environment. The character name I do not want to move from there, but she cannot stay there. Her preferred site after a long time she attains it. Her cognition has a relief, and psychology acquires a chance to talk herself.

When actualises a mirror of herself live, Mr. Sharma comes in his office. The character name I and M both go to the office and ask for an attestation.

Mr. Sharma: Where are your documents?

I: She shows him.

He confers from them.

Mr. Sharma: For what purpose do you need?

I: I am going to apply for a new job.

Mr. Sharma: Can you not self attest?

I: No.

Mr. Sharma: See me.

They transfer documents to Mr. Sharma.

Mr. Sharma: these are photocopies, where are your original documents? I cannot attest without original documents.

I: I have not real documents.

Mr. Sharma: It's a need, you must have original documents.

The character name I asks to M character," Please go home, mom knows where are my documents kept?"

M: What is this? Have you not any responsibility? Do you not know about it? Today I do not want to leave.

I: But I need it, you have to go.

M: Ok, I am going. You sit here and wait.

I: Ok, You come fast.

Meanwhile, a teacher of Maths comes and asks him," Please drop me on the way." A young calculator of the school who has the responsibility of the existing generation. M respects him and shows the expression of honour.

M: Sure.

Now the character name I am alone there. On the right side of my two peons are communicating on the red colour suit. One is an aged male person or other is a female. Female is young, who wears a red suit. Both are gossiping on a red outfit which woman has worn.

Female peon: My suit is in cotton cloth. Is it nice?

Male peon: Yes, Is it pure cotton?

Female peon: Yes.

Male peon: Why do you choose a red colour?

Female peon: I like the red colour.

Male peon: How much cost do you pay for this?

Female peon: Its cost one thousand.

When they listen to each other, their orbs stay on her red purse. I's optic eyes try to make a witness for acquiring permanent tranquillity. At the same time, An old teacher comes from the maths department. Her unconscious serenity takes a brake and sees to him. He sees here and there, and then asks," Whom do you want to meet?

I: I am coming for attestation.

Another teacher: Through expression, he says, "Ok!"

White hair, the height as a high heal and spectacles describe his civilised personality. Another person has gone she still keeps in thoughts.

M the character name has returned with her original documents. He direct goes to clerical office and supplies to Mr. Sharma. Meanwhile, excuse me, sir, May you give me school E-mail Id.

Mr. Sharma: Why?

I: Can we apply through an e-mail?

Mr. Sharma: Yes

I: How much salary can employ get?

Mr. Sharma: Not good get it, a gold medalist employee is getting merely five thousand. You can formulae the standards for the profession.

Both keep silent their feet return to the back. Mr. Sharma is attesting about 20 certificates. They are waiting. When M sees he has to leave today, he decides to message to the owner. But he is only tenth pass then he takes aid from sister. His faulty command on the English language he hands over his phone to sister. She prototypes in the English language. She has an excellent command of English. M does not squeeze out the mean of trying words. So he questions her.

M: What have you typed? Explain to me.

I: I am typing on your behalf today I am unable to move shop due to the anaemic spirit. You seem very excited.

M: No, I am not quite. Have you drafted the message?

I: yes, brother! I have drafted this.

Mr. Sharma: Favour the documents to the principal room for signing. Peon interposes him when he moves to the office. He says," You cannot go inside, therefore, give me, will deliver certificates."

Then he silently returns his seat by sister. Varied shades fluctuate on his face. A little sadness exhibits an idea of back to the drawing board. The character I ask her brother," Now you have much experience in garments." I want to buy a gift for a boy. Please, help me.

M: What type of help do you want?

I: Means, what type of tonal and shades should I buy?

M: Sure like earthy colours pair with tonal light and dark is the best combination. Olive with blues and ochre, blue plus white pair with light beige and navy, orange with greys and blacks, pastels with tonal always.

I: Cross with whom di we pair?

M: In cross-checking check shirts with different bottoms, for everyday work twill checks with core khaki colours pair perfect, linen checks with tonal khakis. Melange checks with solid tonal and checked trousers with neutrals with colours top-wear men look handsome.

I: How does look printed shirts?

M: Printed shirts have a different style. Printed shirts pair with core and coloured khaki. Even printed trousers pair checks, strips, textures tops look dashing.

I: You are so experienced. Do you know the counting of colours? Now tell me," What is the jean wear pair?"

M: Multicolour checks with cargo pants and tinted denim. Polos with mid washed denim the graphic crew with black white denim light washes keep away from direct light and indigos with black denim and core khakis.

I: Excellent! How do you develop your production and brand?

M: Developing brand and production is called a visual merchandising. We engage, attract or motivate the customer towards purchasing this also.

I: Which techniques do you use for developing production and brand?

M: In technical language, we use planogram wall, window display, zoning, merchandise display on wall or floor fixtures(stackings and hangings) mannequin ensemble also.

I: Which are basic techniques?

M: Basic techniques for shirt folding is box folding and paper folding.

I: Are the same criteria to fold T-shirts?

M: No, For T-shirts folding solely A4 sheets use and for crisp folding 2A4 sheets. Hanging, folding, stacking, display, gondola display, seasonal display and for accessory stand have varies techniques. Constructed display wall, planogram wall and Non-planogram wall learn how modifies feet wall use option of shirts or hanging trousers.

I: I have listened about puff folding. What is it?

M: Shirts and T-shirts make a puff fold with logo visible and display it on the wall.

I: Garment line almost depends on the strategy. I did not think so. It means you learn legion keypoints in work.

M: Yes, keypoints help in earning more in a competition like a wall layout should have maximum hanging and less stacking. Emphasis on layering. While layering shirts and T-shirts, all buttons to be kept open, avoid layering contrast colours.

I: What type of fabric are used by Indian companies?

M: Common Indian fabric is slub, satin, poplin, twill, printed, yarn-dyed and dobby textures. These are wovens. Some are knittings.

I: In which options does knitting use?

M: Polo and crews, sweatshirts, and sweaters are knitting fabrics. These options have sub-options also. Some key product concepts clear the confusion of a salesman. He knows about shirt fit and chiselled fit.

I: Do different shirts fit for varies functions?

M: Liberty prints are microfloral or multicolour combinations. Classic oxford for Indian summer solid oxford and coloured yarns are interwoven, Melange fabrics have a wavy effect come, with stretch. Baroque prints use in a soft satin fabrication. Baiadera strips, garments dyed/ pigment Bloch, jacquards and premium linen shirts are also available in 16 different fresh rangings.

I: Do bottom wear have fits varies?

M: Yes, trousers fits have Brooklyn (slim fit), Urban(comfort fit), Kruger(skinner fit) and Kansas(regular fit).

I name character is not reading the intrigue of the day. Her profound psychology is attempting to knowing the code of the day. The secret with amazement is spinning inward. M is showing interest in revealing his knowledge. Iconic khaki plausible in Brooklyn and Kansas fits. Yarn-dyed khaki can wipe. Flight -weight khaki uses for work and travel.

This learning may adopt in future. I am also contemplating to change my career to live a better life. Shaky job and inadequate economic arrangement are undergoing anxiety.

Meanwhile, a ring up someone calls him.

I: Who?

M: A customer.

I: Are you working in a garment shop?

M: Yes.

I: Are you going to deliver any order?

M: No, Do you not know I have joined Rapido?

I: Oh! Good about How many days have you joined Rapido?

M: I joined Rapido last week.

I: How much do you earn?

M: I make three hundred or four hundred rupees at night.

I: Oh! You do only at night, but why?

M: I am serving in a garment store in a day. And Rapido toil runs at night. Today I am a swift flow of water and a glittering of sun rays. So I think my shine must appear in society. My motto is acquired best of both worlds by running muscles. At the drop of a hat can achieve life's gest.

I: The best thing is since sliced bread.

M: Yes.

I: How do you know about Rapido?

M: First of all, I knew from my friend who gave me knowledge about it. Then I logged in this site. I equipped my profile. As I logged in, they messaged me on my phone number. I remembered I got my first message on eleven March. I was so happy because my earning would increase.

I: Rapido is a blessing in disguise.

M: Yes, I have to sing a melodious song.

I: How does Rapido operate?

M: Information technology helps in the capacity as the computer sends a message to the customer and driver. The customer gets the phone number of rider. Customer and driver can call each other and confirm the ride.

I: Can you cancel a ride?

M: Yes, but with strong reason. Because of Illogical reason can give a penalty. A customer can cancel a ride. Hence we can say the ball is in your court.

I: A Rider has loss list instead of hard work.

M: Yes.

I: Is there another way of securing himself?

Yes, when sometime we are in a hurry or another reason we call the customers to cooperate with us.

I: Do you get a salary or commission?

M; Both.

I: How much part you earn and what do they have?

M: Per ride, the Rider executers keep fifteen per cent and rest of the part we have.

I: Who does expand the cost of diesel or petrol?

M: Rider.

I: Ok.

Meanwhile, Principal's office's bell rang, peon goes inside and return with documents. Both are silent and keep eyes on the door. When she places it, a phone rang up. He picks it up to convene from Rapido. He says to her," I have to go and have a ride. I cannot proceed with you. You have to go home alone. I hope you will understand. He has caught between two stools."

She hooks in trouble, But she keeps braveness.

I: Yes, surely.

Both appear out of the office he gets a bike and speeds towards ahead, and She returns home. She responds unrest because she cannot move on a rickshaw because of miserly money. They necessitate a lunch box for going office, But countless moment changes their plan. Now she has not heavy bags strained of playing for a rickshaw. She is very desirous. The hollow of the stomach is waiting for a taste. The nerves and veins are dry for the tasty smell. Even she has outlasted an act of depositing documents on the school reception. Her unrest one part of the brain is in the grip of pessimism while another part of the brain reacts for expectation, the shattered image is unconscious, subconscious. But at last, she hires a rickshaw arrives at home.

Mother: How much time have you contributed there?

I: Clerk was absent today so that we waited there. After half an hour Mr Sharma came then he attested our documents.

Mother: Why have you returned alone? Where is your brother?

I: He got a call for a ride. A customer was waiting. Mother, forget all job make for the empty stomach. Listen to me my abdomen has shrunk flat like a balloon.

Mother: It seems as you have sunk. I have prepared lunch, have lunch and need rest. I will do all.

I: No, after lunch I will go to another school for applying. Then I will take relief.

When she was having lunch, her brother arrives home. Tiredness glimpse on his face also but available for her sister's sustenance. Before going out of the home, he takes a cup of coffee she covered her face with green dupatta.

M: Where are we going?

I: We will go to a public school.

M: What is the name of the school?

I: Shiv Shakti Public School.

M: Where is it located? I have forgotten all the route to my city.

I: Near the railway track of senior secondary school it is located.

M: Yes, where should I move after crossing?

I: Crossing the railway track you have to move the right side in the second street. In the end, you can perceive the school board.

M: Whenever I misremember, please direct me.

She is nervous and thinking," How would she answer in front of them? A little unconscious brain threatens her innate spirit for an unpredictable future." He is astonished on his psychological schemes which have transformed with the time. Life's exhausted coronavirus swallows the healthy brain. It seems each brain needs quarantine for long and healthy. Both have arrived. He sets a bike on the side while she asks peon for the reception. He guides to the left side. She enters the acceptance.

I: Good afternoon, mam.

Receptionist: Very pleasant midday, mam, and what can I do?

I: I want to apply for a job.

Receptionist: Deposit your original self-attested documents, application and experience. Tell me your marks of metric, graduation and master degree.

I: She passes information of metric, graduation but forgets marks of Master Degree. It appears her face has painted white. His stressful pons has lost memory. She keeps silent for a moment, puts a hand on the head and closes her eyes. After a minute she says estimated marks to the receptionist. She feels stress-free as soon as she passes documents.

The first day of LOCKDOWN is full of enthusiasm. This day is thinking about the holidays. Each citizen shock with a sudden announcement of captivation in the home nobody kens how many days they have to live as aboriginal. The children meet with father who had not to time for the family before. The first LOCKDOWN is for ten days. Adolescence boys are busy with mobile. Each home has a noise of LCD, a full day cacophony. Each wall has struck of colours' cry. Women's days routine has changed. Even family's getting time has also switched on the announcement of LOCKDOWN. But the picture of the Indian market has a risk form. LOCKDOWN has transformed the inner rest into the fear of saver LOCKDOWN. Hoarding of essential commodities has moved into the black marketing. While the government is proposing for pleasing to the public, the psychological approach of bodies is denting the scarcity of basic things. For applying victoriously, LOCKDOWN needs hard steps cops are marching and announcing for shutting down the whole market. The increasing responsibility of the police and anxiety of people make a draft of equilibrium. The social distancing as the corner of the chessboard is solely the triumph of alive lives. Chaos replaces the tranquillity on the arriving of the police people, move into the home the sounds of horns has a habit of an anvil. Men have unexpected leaves with the cold ear. But women have trapped in taste. Although some home men are carrying the responsibility of caring for children, some wicked furore husbands have become a hemicrania for women. Just so an image, I am going to present before you a ten members family who is an epitome of society. Grandfather, grandmother, two sons, two daughters-in-law and their children are enjoying at home. Even Grandparents help in shouldering children spending quality time.

Grandmother: We are lucky, sons respect us in society who are holding at home lightly bet. Mother should pray for children for progressing future. The environment of the world has swallowed the honour of senior citizens. But we bless from god so never evade this grace. What my sons do not like to do I dodge that for calmness, they keep us on the convenience platform.

Ingredients of kitchen smell the home, tempering of spices increase the belly void. A childish manner of men in LOCKDOWN forms the capacity of consciousness. A chess game, ludo, cricket match devotion for god at both time of day and singing a song in a loud voice are the sources of roasting time. It seems to bless and curse both borrow from infinity. Bless is quality time for each unavailable family. Authorities who have a void of deep strength of the relationship this quality time is making more aromatic. There is no worry of the economic state, but the poor and middle-class family have seasoning need. This financial status influences directly on women society. Here rank controls their hands-on daily expenditure. On the position of women, they are not easy even in blockade country. But TERRACE wanders alone for a long time today have a lot of flowers. A sound of giggling, playing, screaming, fighting, chirping, the sound of homonyms clattering with the walls all are in the lap of the terrace. The loneliness of the terrace's wall has fainted like a whitewash. Neighbours have time for discussion from the terrace balcony. Gossip is a part of the daily routine. Meanwhile, someone notices the clearance of clouds where layers of dust were governing its rules. The clouds have flourished the colour of nebulae.

Other cons of zero use of petrol and diesel work as a purifier of the atmosphere and standard level of health. Science has taken in the place of mythology. Everyone has prepared to accept the pill of science. Media plays the role of a globule. Media awakens to people for liveliness. Saving a life is on the floor of gest. Life can see KARMA. Everyone has a cast for an act of KARMA. Aid is everywhere for the more economic sector. The support of raw and cooked food as Langar is sweet for necessitates. Half closed shops is a curtain on the restriction of government for some time for controlling the public. Social distancing due to LOCKDOWN is pausing the rap cases as well as accidents. Girls are living as birds. The girls are flying in the sky or demons captivate in the grip of coronavirus's cell. The zero use of vehicles presents zero results of accidents. The white shadow of the sun can easily see on the roads than the end. Cops and doctors are washing to the society building. Cleanliness servants are in the kind of HIT which is hitting the unpleasant bugs caller, Who are surviving endangering living, high workshop grants them to quarantine for the family community shelter. The growth of the epidemic is pulling society ten years back. Unemployment virus is covering the footings.

Ancestors home is a sheltered paradise. Maini family's two brothers who are different from each other, elder brother who earns ten thousand in a shop as a helper but does not like to handle his shop, as a helper he is happy to make a hand of wealth, and three sisters who are married. A young brother who makes love marriage a girl works in the same field. Vijay and Bhavi both earn the same range of salary. They earn forty thousand a month live a high level of life than the elder brothers family. Mother-in-law of Bhavi has a shop on rent. Second level clothes for the poor and middle family is a trend of making. A contribution has made by mother-in-law for years. She has a large aiding to grocery, vegetables, milk. Conclusively, Mrs. Bhatia is a foundation stone of Bhatia's family. Elder brother and his wife both are illiterate. But their attitude is like a lion. Because of lack of space younger brother and his wife buy a separate home, careless behaviour for their child they take a comprehension step, ignorance their child due to biased expression, this home is a heaven for them. Mother-in-law lives with a younger brother and his wife in a new home. Authority of an old home elder brother and his family make power. But a mythological and orthodox mirror's image can undoubtedly recognize. Reema mother has one son and one daughter, but her move towards the son. Son wandering the street while a girl has the stressed of getting ninety per cent marks, Reema has a limited expectation from a girl. She wants her daughter to earn with study in insufficient food. Unstoppable schedule per day crushes her body into small pieces. Study solemnise from four o'clock to six o'clock, body refreshes in one hour, seven to eight-thirty tuitions by foot about twelve miles faraway then college nine to four o'clock, after turning tips tuition to children. Yet the mom has a desire for an energetic cuisine with ingredients in the evening road's group invites her for continuing gossiping. Bones describe the short story of a prejudice mom. She screams against inhumanity before legion desires.

Mother: Shut up! You are not only trained in education. Yet your study is inadequate do not discover me.

Shiksha: You give me a cup of milk while brother a full of glass of milk, why?

Mother: He is a boy. He is sunshine of the home. He will grow our dynasty, but you will go from here.

Shiksha: The whole work is done by he does not adequately read and spent the entire day out. Why do you collapse my rights with him? Where are his duties?

Mother: You just focus on your study. Do not rubbish. Do what he wants. I am your mother while you are not. He will home handle while you will move to another home. He should physically strong. You have not distinctive quality.

Shiksha: Why do you study me?

Mother: You should help your father. He has not satisfactorily salary.

Shiksha: Why should I? Why do you not say him? If he the home handler, he should help father.

Mother: Observe neighbour's daughter how much she works hard. She supports her father in unfortunate situations. Even she does not get married in forty years ago.

Shiksha: You are a mean sacrifice for me. I must serve and sacrifice for family. And he should relish without any act. Your partial behaviour makes qualify than him. It means I am your bank. He runs farthest as roads invite him and appear roads have depressed without him.

Mother: Her face is scorching like the sun. Her ego is an epitome of Ravan who burnt his dynasty in his stubborn and blindness. Mother is playing the character of hostility for a daughter.

Shiksha: Mother is not a mother. I am not opposed to your but your thoughts. You are also a human being. I am somewhat younger than you although I know KARMA is superior to relationships, how I acknowledge you, KARMA is a base of life. You could help father if you did not leave a job. You cannot do a job or run a shop. Shiksha's pain with confidence shine on her face. Both are standing in the room which has a sofa on the left hand on the entrance. And on the right side a bed for rest, in the centre of the left and right side an old T.V has placed which describes the story of the last two decades. This room depicts the tale of a hard work girl. A girl who is an abstract of power feels herself like a cucumber, whose fluid give cool and fairness. For some time a dark spot inside but a smile returns on the face for bright future. Sharp-pointed nose, gluey cheeks, sticky body demonstrate an illustration of poverty and self-obsessed mother. Insufficiency and favouritism like coronavirus have a phobia in every second and every relationship.

Scepticism virus

An alcoholic head of mohalla named Darsi who is married has three children. His marriage is unstable due to alcohol. A long tunnel of stigma is covering his marriage relationship. He has an interest in politics. Diplomacies, where is not any favour to reach, is a black burqa. The diplomacy of intelligence where the bond always on exposure, an art of playing with other sentiments is a game of governing. The cruelty of politics in the form cop will perceive easily. Today institutions expose its money-minded politics. Employees in the institutions are the carbon copy of the politics of their owners. In the market also screen a politics of black marketing. Mohallas do not remain without politics because of like Darsi people. Darsi means efforts while whom I am talking here he is efforting to collecting a store of alcohol like a camel. Despite all, he knows of computer techniques which is a source of income. He operates computers for printing the colouring on the small white pieces. Some times on the portrait pages and landscape pages. Cotton tactility hard palette of keyboards with the light of spectacles. His cerebrum has puzzled in rudiments on desire profession. But his marriage has a taste of the sauce. The feud between them due to alcohol has become a social gossip.

Hence a woman of a street itches his wife who comments ironically on her," Do not jealous whole day." His wife does not utter any word with a faint face return. Before this, she was discussing her daughter's intelligence.

" My small daughter is intelligent in English. She knows the basics of grammar well. She knows how to write a topic within two to three minutes and so have not to worry about her future."

In reality, her husband insults her to catch her daily routine. He manifests her in society. His words cross the acceptance limits of husband and wife. Ten years of marriage relationships have converted a part of people's gossip. Anxiety seems in behaviour and attitude but does not leave alcohol. One day he sits outside of the shop which is not his. His friend who welds a drunker his wife stitches clothes. His friend's elder brother's wife is a prostitute. Darsi snickers in his company being a peacock. Alcohol trumpets the death alarm. The demon has become a part of the economy. The government interdictions for a formality due to powering economy is impossible to demolish the production of alcohol. Where is stock, there is a value. Darsi sits alone outside the shop while a woman comes out. She is sixty years old, but her appearance of forty-five. She has dedicated her life to the family pleat neck has killed her soul cycle. While her eyes are observing vendors for daily needs. Darsi calls her and blames.

A woman does not express her mental distress by saying any word.

Woman: What happens, son?

Darsi: My mother-in-law is a louse who always suck my blood. Like a housefly, she is spreading a pandemic from a murky area of healthy food. My wife does not follow me. My mother-in-law has snatched my nap. My wife's tongue mists of chilly I always yearn for love. We always baffle. My wife's psychology derives with the remote of mother-in-law's brain.

What should I do?

You should keep her heart with love.

Woman: What do you do?

Darsi: I am Publisher.

Woman: I think you do another job also. Am I right?

Darsi's face fades. He surprisingly thinks how she knows my politics mask. Perhaps people tell her.

Woman: How many glasses do you drink today?

Darsi: Hysteria. I never fall in digs of roads like drinkers.

Woman: You are also drunker whether you take less or more. The drug is a drug. Because of the drug, you have grown nefarious. A wife feels shame. Why do you not concede this? Your pill hurts children.

Darsi: I take two or three pegs a day.

Woman: Two or three pegs are enough for impairment.

Darsi: In politician society, the drug is essential for the company. She should adjust with husband although she ignores me I am attempting to leave it. I am not only a husband but also a man.

Woman: Rumination is a process of consciousness. Your subconsciousness is not allowing to the aware soul. I know you are a man or you can not blind himself. She is attempting to leave the co-wife drink. Can I give you a suggestion?

Darsi: Yes.

Woman: Says yes, always whatever she says. If she does not like to drink, you will not touch. I promise she will never be displeased with you.

Darsi: She will. I am sure even she does not like to politics. One day I said to her," Come with me in Gurudwara for a Political leader." But she ignored and said," She does not like political gatherings." I requested her though she did not go inside. She threatened me," She would return home on foot." As soon as I listened, I entered inside wordlessly. I felt feeble before her.

Darsi's eyes and facial expression full of the strain he asks her again what should I do?

Woman: Simple says," yes." always whatever she says. Imagine every day is a LOCKDOWN day. I am sure to drink will leave. Forcing power is a bigger dam between both of relation. Compelling her means breaking period. The cache value of her desires should first responsibility yours. Your "Yes" is heaven for survival. Darsi goes from here with profound thoughts. A woman returns home with a question," Are all accounts same?" She has not a life of sweet sugar candy.

A reflector of have-not always presence in thoughts. Nature is screaming against the exploitation of natural resources, the holiness of woman, inhumanity and unfaithful relationships. Nature is locking to squeal of humanity. This attempt will take legion death. The red stain of a virus is a danger of destruction. Exploitation is burning in the red zone. The virus is breaking the chain of imps who accept a woman is a weaker sex. The virus is exposing the truth of husband and wife relationships. The depth of the father and mother in the walls of the home becomes a training scaffold for children.

A time for understanding the sensitivity of families is a greater responsibility. Migrants have become a responsibility of state government. Tribals are also a part of society though no one has focused on them. Tribals are using leaves for securing her breath. It seems the virus is indicating and threatening us," He has to destruct the whole world. Whether a human has developed in the laboratory or advertised by the human, I am brute will not omit you."

Abstemiousness

This virus cannot suppress corruption. Whether depravity of synthetic material or partial red-handed society. Entertainment studio is cheering from the house. Information and technical communication sector are promoting to complete process of the administration. Dance, music and gym videos are entertaining people through ITC. ITC has boon outcomes stand by also. Machinery is keeping control over us or however, we can say we are under the control of it. We are hunting by profound politics which keeps an eye on us we are unaware of the demon. Even we are losing our consciousness from relationships. Our bound state of mind is losing an existent environment due to the closeness of electronic evidence. Less exercise of physical activities is dying a healthy appearance of a human. Nutritional relationships are the link to human society. Eyes have forgotten the real objects and as fingers have lost the soft touch. Vertebral and shoulders have bent before the time. The strain of light if electronic gadgets have scorched the shine of the skin. The book of life inquires in shrewd politics. Even starving part of society determines a large part of the wealth of the ITC sector. A chronic intrusion of developing craftmanship on social aptitude which has locked human activities. Sun transfers relief in winter but burns in summer same as ITC is adding in pandemic world. Death is the consequence of LOCKDOWN, and it proves today's human can not live a captive life. Limited liberty has defiled patience power. Penury is real wealth and poor hero of the country they are fighting before disappearing enemy.

The character of M is paying services in LOCKDOWN. M character has spent almost twenty-five days at home with enjoying varies dishes. Movies and nap in the day are decorating his leisure time. After twenty-five days, his consciousness arises anxiety for future stress.

M: How much do I watch the movie?

I: Focus on your study. It's a golden period for you. If you use it accurately, it will surely reward you. The degree is the demand of your promotion. Life learns you through the deductive method. Time is giving a chance to learn a psychosocial.

M: My brain is running on the path of assembling capital. Now the study is the second world for me. Mall's owner is crediting in three parts of one month salary. FIVE THOUSAND, FIVE THOUSAND, FIVE THOUSAND! Do you get the March salary?

I: Yes, they called me yesterday.

M: Are they deduct salary?

I: No.

M: Someone tells me cop is releasing job. I want to apply. Someone knows me I am requesting to him.

I: Will the current crowd help you?

M: Sure. He is the head of mohallas who is sustaining to the public. He goes with exuberance the excuse is there. The ration is the symbol for wandering outside. The tricks compel eyes to bend down before uttering the false talk. Bend eyes explore his inner soft. The narrow street of life has moved in the slum fields. Large eyes traverse from heart's communication. Afternoon time does not dare to stop him like parents. Mother is a half- decorated antique piece who listens to them. M believes in her but, does not leave the filthy company. His passion breaks the chain of the captivity of safety. When he returns after distributing the ration, he meets to the head of the mohallas. He sits outside the red zone areas of the virus with cops.

Darsi: From where have you come?

M: Public service.

Darsi: Oh!

M: I also want to join this service force.

Darsi: What do you do here? Full day standing ovation in the scorching sun is a tension of service. You will glow in bravery service.

M: I will. You just sign me rest way I will complete.

Darsi: Wait, will see. I will call you tomorrow.

M: Will expect.

He returns in forty-five minutes. And asks mother I met Darsi just last five to ten minutes before. He sat outside the red zone section. I said to him for joining this force. Hopefully, I will go tomorrow. The yellow lights come out from the clouds. Scattering the rays of sun on the world's face are knocking the door of the human consciousness. But Darsi's sentience lost in whiskey's bottle which crosses the face in the mirror. Meanwhile, M character sun is knocking to move from the walls. The first day's cop's training is full of determination and courage.

Cop: Verbal communication should first deal, do not kick anyone. Patience and piece are armour in a horrible situation. Take a stick for making a distance between person to person for securing the effect of the pandemic. The exclusive way to deprive the epidemic is a distance.

M: I do not need a wooden stick. A wooden armour will not safe me while it will cut my hand.

Cop: What?

M: Means my wrath is boundless. No one can evaluate my rage range. A wooden stick will create a LAXMAN REKHA, So keep it bay. M has burned in the sun, but hunger does not die in the heart. Meanwhile, a person comes with chemical cold drinks, but no one touches them. Cops offer chilled chemical water to M, but he also ignores. M's face tells the tale of his tiredness. Air-conditioner person has jumped on the bandwagon that is why he is drinking the yellow drink. A woman from the red zone hot spot comes out from home for buying medicines.

Cop: Go back, or else I have to hard in behaviour. Fourteen days are an essential part of your life. We are not responsible though you have driven all in the dangerous grip. A little passion was the key to liberty.

Near cop M also requests her for quarantine. He says to her," A doctor will come for a check-up then." M is a butter hearted. He is melting to see worse conditions of beings. His psychology perceives with eyeballs and feels with senses. Nature has the horsepower to punish people. Then a sergeant returns from duty, he stands up for census for area. At the same time, a companion guides him," sit here. Data will collect from a medical team contrarily the corona gift will honour you." The first sergeant convenes again with gloom. The horror of death reflects in khaki. Doctors, nurses, cops, sweepers and pharmacist all are the representation of redemption while ignorance and carelessness are a letter of release. The first day ends with suggestions. At home, he repeats the whole day conversation aloud as a drape in his guilt. In the night scene, the neighbour maintains a silent until he explains the entire day. The route has changed, the net day morning brings a novel tale. In the daylight of the dark of the room, he sleeps on the folding bed in the drawing-room. His late morning awakes with a ring of the phone. The comparison in services which is a training of PUNJAB police in the belief of future has confidence for a higher authority. He retains a harmless distance from a bacillus by selecting a duty hour. His nap awakes with the din of social media. Whenever his companion suggests him, he ignores.

Lethargy

He does not go to the police station from attendance. His companion goes and calls him for arriving on duty. A lobby touches the border of the bathroom, which is a place of relaxing property of two hours a roadside window meets the world clutch a tranquil. Meaningless calls which have only one constancy to acquire salary notice a soring of time is flying the ash of requirements. The horror is rushing in senses of M. Time changes with the zone of the area. People are flutter then cops have a single suggestion to live at home. When they do not follow the rules, they cut the Challan.

Cop: People will not accomplish healthy lockdown on account of agitation action. We do not know wherewith they will feel to appreciate self-safety.

Meanwhile, a well-wisher comes with banana service. DSP asks a female sergeant to distribute bananas.

Female sergeant: Sir, please take it first to you.

DSP: NO. You take it.

Female sergeant: With a smile, you are showing fear of the virus. Am I right?

DSP: No. The heart is ignoring banana yet. Do not think so. Give me one for your satisfaction.

The female sergeant is distributing one by one with a smile and teasing to everyone on saying," Take coronavirus!"

Female sergeant: She comes by M and asks for a banana until he refuses. All laugh on her dialogue. Does not threat It's coronavirus take it one.

Ferocity and desperation

Ferocity and desperation is a consequence of coronavirus. Political parties attain the trophy to lock the city. Fierceness has transformed into despair. In a lockdown, despondency is a fire candle which is burning everyone. An eminent and wealthy person cooks in the depression oil. A needful personality vanishes into the hang of nature. Even a lack of police and fulfilling the area's knowledge build a chain of volunteers. Enlistees are in trouble when they bust a gut to revive saviour in troublesome conditions. Missionaries hold a charge of checking on chowk media raise questions. Media reporter of T.V channel 'Investigator Web' records live news of volunteers and says," See how Law enforcement officers retain rest and Volunteers are investigating the original and mandatory documents in critical contingence. How irresponsible Law enforcement agency for the country safety? Without a helmet, people are passing nearby the long arm of the law neglect for continuing the concatenation of corruption. Police are disturbing law and order for increasing self-importance. The police officers are ignoring public to gain. Public unawareness expands the way of earning."

As the reporter explains the particular life, polis reaches front for common inspect. Sooner or later media holds the sound of air jet in the clouds which do not appear. Unexpected assault of presence arises their soul on duty. Two volunteers in each corner are reviewing the public than two police officer do their job on the seeing of media reporter. Two officers are cancelling challan moreover other four polis stand nearby sitting officers. Some people are passing without investigation. The reporter is shouting against the partial attitude of corruption, and that time Law administration officers attack the charge of mental harassment on duty.

Polis: Media is disturbing us. They do not make us converge on our job. Channel is torturing and blaming wrong.

Meanwhile, assistants ring in the main branch. Procrastinating SI arrives, and he asks a reporter," From which newspaper do you belong? Why do you disturb them on duty?

The reporter does not answer. People gather on the road, and all officers fix there.

SI: Do you know the law? First, read the law then asks us a question. Law gives permission helper in hard circumstances. Ordinary people have the right to secure the public when he/ she sees someone in trouble. Volunteers are our helper in stiff conditions. Government selects them for our help, and these missionaries are not our choice person. Then a female officer claims against a reporter that he is here for a purpose to free his member whom we have arrested last day for the law-breaking on the road. We will never leave him until he pays charges according to lockdown law. A reporter appeal on channel polis is trying to divert the topic for securing themselves. While officers go on duty, people pass from the road towards their aim. M is also a Volunteer. After seeing the scene on the path, he feels disturbed mentally. He came to buy a bag of flour. He is returning with thoughtful insight. M is thinking about his rights as an assistant of legitimacy. He gets news of those areas where a case of coronavirus has engulfed the seven members of a family. His duty has transformed the mentality of M. An image of anger and desperation of hunger and diplomacies! Between two parties and for self profit a market plays chess in a pandemic. In the evening time, doctors with ambulance and police stimulate the media for the latest news. Municipality showers the alcohol-based chemical. All bugs move around the epidemic family. Police announce to personages," Live at home. No one can come outside until the reports of all tests in hands. Legal army prohibits the mobile movie even on the terrace. But how it can possible media does not take a glimpse in a man's life. As mechanisms expose the lights on the epidemic family, a man yells against his family's protection.

Man: We are not adds. Do not make spices for the world's entertainment. It's common as other diseases. Media is unveiling before the public as we hung in crime. If the agency does not halt to live coverage on T.V, my family will commit suicide.
As the word of suicide alerts the medical team as well as the law protector, they raise a safety circle around the man and his family. When the sun loses scorching power in the evening five-thirty, today people are watching the show free on the roads. When even like cases expose media humanity dies, the souls yells for a respectable life. The witness reporters are snubbing the right of living with freedom then a man moves his steps ahead for hugging the reporter. M apprehends the losing identity in the society for the time being the change. A man's eyes are getting the load as a sinner of community. Here man's ego and respect stand on the shore of the ocean where he will drown or come out with his logical confidence. Man's proceeding onward paces mounts the fear of a pandemic, and they tread toward the outside of the street. Now the reporters are running from that area for securing awe of clinging the disease. A man is calling and saying," Come, make a video, earn money from our advertisement as terrible news. I am waiting, Why are you not make a grip on the breaking news for your channel? I am not different from you. We are same just a newly sickness gripping caught me, and this is the best way to earn more, Come, take a click, and you will popular with me."

Darsi and M both are gawking to check out on live news. M has analytical views about the diplomatic community. M recognises the hoodwink on the name of humanity, which is mocking the human globally and participating in arising the demons. Media's cruel intention stand him before alliances like From where did you hold under control in this epidemic? Whom did you meet per day? Where did you go? Media, army and doctors all are detectives besides the spoiler on the retired decent post. The reporters hide in another road for escaping themselves back-stabbing. Law administrator officers again announce to the public," Go inside, No one lives even on the terrace, human expect humanity than a global joke. Encourage them for better returning with family. Morally and mentally improvisation is an essential motivation. Media reporters also show their supremacy before patients." Then polis and doctors receive them in the ambulance. As they ahead of the whole area disinfect with alcoholic chemical, people bind for twenty-one days. Going outside roads are now blocked with bamboo and ropes. Law protector deputies with volunteers of that area inquire day and night. Darsi and M live each other's opposite road, and appointees of government are guarding to that region on the main street. Darsi and M both assist them on the weapon-based conditions. In every critical situation, polis calls him for reconciliation among people. Their unbiased eye polaroid catches the images of irregular wanderers and suggests to Darsi for requesting people to keep inside. He instructs people with political activities.

As a volunteer M also supervises them, Darsi runs political encephalon. But both fail to establish tranquility when opposition parties tangle with the common man on the daily routine. A group of minorities has been living for five years. In the evening time, Darsi's opposite party's member pays duty as a volunteer alongside from quad minority person comes outside for bathing. And then blue turban wear volunteer warns him for going inside although he does not bother, and blue turban man's anger explores in a loud voice. He takes a bath and leaves inside then another migrant leaves the room for taking a shower. A female officer stops him for doing so yet he returns an answer in misbehave manner, a blue turban man is watching all. Then till he returns in an officer send him with another volunteer for comprehending the rules of the government. Rough language and high temper turban-wearing man sudden assaults on migrants Vagabonds snatch his beard and turban and throw on the ground. A crowd of mortals encompass them for leaving inappropriate subjugation, explosive criteria of man. A turban man in rage beats with a stick on his head and break the bones of the vertebra. That time a political person is planning to publish the news on channels. A nearby man who makes a movie on the mobile camera gives threat. No one knows who has produced the proof. Darsi who is cyclically roaming the news is on the exploitative layout, and he wants to take revenge from turban man. Darsi agitates globe-trotters for making pressure on turban man. His policy craves to leaning before himself so that he demands help to him. Darsi excites rovers for casting a case against turban man. In the night's curtain, Darsi plays a dangerous game for fulfiling animus in which turban man has not to skill of statecraft. But Darsi's day and the night spent in artfulness for bowing him at any cost.

Meanwhile, the leader of vagabonds files a case of attempting murder. Polis had already warned all volunteers not to beat people without any reason. When they see the matter in the fire, the police tries to calm both sides. From the backside, Darsi gives suggestion migrant admit in hospital for acquiring more money from turban man. Under pressure, he will pay either he will proceed to Darsi for agreement. His great loot traverses his demon who is the malicious cynosure of wills, a camouflage appearance of the evil has a void of the popularity. His tactic design arrives on the peak when legal authority set back in the form of disagreement. Turban man raises a question to come forward female officer whom with migrants have misbehaved. Police refuse by saying that she is on holiday and a female officer is still a trainer. Turban man in an aggressive manner throws backfires of malicious words each one. Officers are attempting to spoil this matter with the agreement. When legal men estimates of throwing firestone each other and no one turns towards the contract. Police take back steps and say they are not responsible for all worst situations. They threat turban man also for exchanging views. A turban man does not aspire for paying cash while he is ready to fight a court case. Everyone is trying to persuade him not to uphold the trial. Officer and M also consider him that you are wrong, you snatched the migrants from their quad and started the abusive fight and so that he should accept their accession. Finally, before migrants revolution turban man pays the ten thousand amount.

The other shade of spirit of Darsi is as a husband ignorable role. He deems that a woman needs only supplies. It does not matter how and from where a man accumulates. According to Darsi statement, a woman is a materialistic personality who does not pursue the man's desires. A woman solely converges the home's essentials. For a woman, a man is a luxury for living a better life. One day Darsi arrives M's home for reaching another place of political issues. It's a morning time about eight-thirty when he meets his mother outside the apartment in a hurry. While M is playing the game on the phone in a relaxed position, then Darsi sudden jump in front of him after taking blessings from his mother. M's father lies in the middle of the corridor Darsi wishes him and alerts M for getting ready in five to ten minutes, and then till Darsi receives a call and wait for him in the drawing-room. Mother is preparing tea for Darsi, and father is talking with Darsi ill-mannered. I character is serving with mother. Disorderly home's picturesque illustrate the daily morning's routine. Darsi sits in the drawing-room attempt to chat with his father.

Darsi: Uncle, nowadays you are not talking with me. Why?

Uncle: You do not keep steps on the moralistic way. So that I am not interested in talking with you

Darsi: Can you tell me the unethical trails taken by me?

Uncle: You do not do any exclusive upright effect. Which can I explain?

Darsi: Leave it, uncle.

M has come from washroom after taking a bath, and now Darsi holds a fanfaronade before his family for exposing his position in the political field. On the return of his boastfulness M's father insults him by saying," First, you should establish yourself in society." Darsi again repeats his brag by saying," He will raise M's status in the community. Very soon M will have the position of Inspector, and He will surely earn fifty thousand per month. Hence you will not require to do work."

As his father overhears this brag, he reacts with an egocentric and humorous laugh on him.

Uncle: First, you should inflate your rank then feed others.

Darsi 's furore erects on his insulting drive. As the mother notices the volcano of fire almost ejaculating range, she changes the topic for serving the cold environment.

Mother asks Darsi," Have you known any correction officer in the correction centre? Actually on my Aadhaar card age has written wrong. Can you say someone for correction of age? I need to spring my pension. Now, I have my granddaughter also so that I require cash. For household purposes, the son's income is not enough, and even my daughter is unable to earn due to lockdown, and we have not any other sources. If you can do something, I will still in favour of you in future. Darsi: Aunty, You should say to uncle. I have heard that uncle have a high-quality personality who can do only in a second. Why did you not do, uncle?

All keep silent because they know uncle is faulty. M character has completely bend from inner on account of father's worst active role. He diverts the topic and says to Darsi for going. They have gone just his mother's hatred burst on the husband.

Mother: I know you do not aspire your children grow in community. Why do you not leave us alone? Why are you spoiling your children's gist? They have a little life, and you have not right to block their paths. You did not do anything for their long list, and you have not earned cash even respect even today you are merely spending life on excuses. Ghosting rent will die their future do not construct a border for hanging.

Father: Darsi is not a good guy. And you should pivot on son. He is a political leader who knows to make a grip on the young generation.

Mother: Because of you my son is in bad company. If you collected require things at a young age, you would not work now. Keep in your sense. I shall never pardon you if my children reduce dust under you. It is misdeed even to see your face. It is all your doing due to children are facing uncertainty. I solely waste my time with you. You should feel ashamed.

Son has returned at ten' clock and being he enters, he does a shower. A man before the family shows care and ignorance of another male. A man exhibits more knowledge before the family and another man's inferior slice. A man's self slice is sweeter than other males.

M: He is not so good so as soon as possible overlook him. He has two children though he links outsider woman. He knows the weakness of people and then uses it. Idiot he is attempting to reopen the file case against turban man. I keep silent. Try to ignore him.

Mother takes breakfast, and he takes a ride towards his destiny. Now home's ambience transforms into quietness. He attends alarm of one spin to school. A female employee who is going to collecting a salary, money is more powerful. Taking a ride in the sweltering morning between spreading pestilence M gets an opportunity to intercept a job for his sister I.

M: Is there any vacancy?

Customer: Not now. Send resume if they need, they will call. Vacancies vacant suddenly they call. Lockdown is a funk of famine, and even higher authority has a phobia of the poverty line. Now we are on the death line who knows when they will announce.

Her destiny has on the peak and M on the returning move. M turns a strange path where the government has prohibited on account of several accidents. M has interested in miracle and mysterious places. He runs a ride on the mystery. His motility is in the venture to divert the lines of the map. A high road from where a turned cut in the left side, a far distance a middle circle has an enigma of disappearing of people. As he deviates the left, wind trend blows in horrific compressed. A dark drift of clouds brings thunder which is bumping in the back foot. He can acknowledge the mysterious truth what he has listened to a feeling of someone there. Someone is cracking his bike from the back foot and take the following place screaming in his hearing, moreover, he watches behind there is not anyone. As he arrives in the circle, his bike does not work. A halt before forwarding a human but why his brain does not run, as seems hard disk has almost cracked. And the scenes have vanished from the screen, handling the bike has become a crucial task. Evaporate images retain sects to propel the back. He ventures to stand the two-wheeler and looks around for a while. Which power is halting to passengers ahead and why? But nothing is there. As he takes a trace leading, the thundering disaster shifts backwards. One hour mysterious quest does not give a sign of taking life. The death agreement does not haunt nevertheless does not give away of going. Unprotected way browbeats him for proceeding backwards. He does not get then ultimately his hands turn and foot bullies to follow the path from where he entered. Brain shocks and lips are murmuring to the unseen revelation still a threat is inside the fist of heart. Exactly contemplating thought arouses a riddle he stays in front of the home. On the day's result, the sun is bitting with the sharp rays teeth and thought process is itching the cerebrum. Mother makes lemon water.

The rain of questions: How do you spend your day? Do you have earned or not? Will you go later? The shades of the colour have demolished in the itching day-star.

M: Hun. A few time, I want my quarantine time for running smoothly. I badly need a respite from all stresses.

Mother: She takes a long breath, and says oK.

M: I relish the sense of sovereignty the time offer that I never experienced in my life before. And what other people sense as detention do the opposite to me. It gives me freedom. I am far from the pressure of slavery questions. I open the eyes to the requirement that helps in a pandemic. My senses hurl the fear and nervousness from thoughts. And my self-centred approaches sleep in the corner, a sudden reminiscence of unveiling the mystery pause. After relaxation, He resumes ability and positivity, a cup of tea dive fresh the garnish mind. This incident brings improvement in responsibility.

In about two hours, he finds himself in a passionate ambience. But he does not forget his business to mystery acquisition. Because of good memory, he bargains of his daily routine, and he gets success attaining the goal. Turned his psychology in the appearance of regular works in the peer groups, he communicates among peer groups on the side of the road. The volunteers and officers are discussing on household matters and manifest the ultimatum on revealing the strength of the disease. Government has gesticulated hands before the epidemic. The various efficacious and curvacious countries have bent their knees. Reverberation public should make a distance from a touchable attacker besides cremation would not suffice. Hospital staff merely hang on the luke water and paracetamol medicine. Friend, we do not go even inside the home outside the apartment take food and sleeps in the corridor. The infection has lost the quietness of thinking power. Then one officer asks for tea, M comes home and says to mother for preparing ten cups of tea with all stuff of spices like cardamom, cloves, ginger, cinnamon. But how he will serve them because a tea stewpot is not attainable. Mother commands for a kettle and rupture on husband's lofty attitude. They are living in the lower level of poverty. He asks Darsi Do you have a tea kettle? But he gets 'No'. Mother keeps the 'Dolu' in front of him and asks Dolu is a symbol of inadequacy and ability of both son and father. He brings disposable glass for having tea. His unnecessary expenditure is loading future. M rotates towards on his path and the taste of home tea fresh their brain and makes demands of tea more.

Now their day and evening have passed furthermore all have gone home merely M and one officer on duty. The other will respond after dinner till M is placing stuff of loneliness. After one hour another officer handles recognition to liability, M now goes home for a banquet. As he goes ahead on each step he seems, someone is following without the sound of walking. Five minutes for a home isolate him on the road and whispers the horror vibrations in the ears. M is running it through the mind and trying to find a way to turn it so that it all sounds quite natural. A mystery arouses the insight strength for searching it. His destiny is in the walk, and mother sits outside the home for waiting. As her vision shot him, she stands, goes in the kitchen for preparing food. He removes the shoes outside the porch and sprays the shower of alcoholic chemical. M direct goes to the bathroom for blossoming the body freshness. After having a bath, he walks in the drawing-room to feasting himself. Mother slices of salad in a plate, a sweet of milk in a dish, a bowl of vegetable and pours a glass of lemon water. A full large plate has rushed his void in the hollow stomach. After taking a meal, he watches T.V, calling receives for getting knowledge of his job. Night twelve's clock he closed the T.V, and he takes petite footprints onto the stairs. Going upward direction subconscious is chit-chatting of mystery walk behind himself last two hours. The sky is darkening more, and it is getting hot. He looks up and down the cool breeze is trying to touch his burning hull. He closes his eyes in the hanging ventilation for feeling again the invisible case whatever would happen if he locks the scary reminiscence.

The intelligence of mind has blocked the block of murmuring the solution of the veiling story. He moves back down to the sleeping room. Later, he walks back to the kitchen for taking a glass of water. His eyes gawk to watch on the wall, and he squats on his couch. He sprawls on the right side, bending the arm under the head on the bed, and later he holds his lips in the tight line. M opens his eyes and lit the light of the room and sits again on the pot. M stands and moves outside in the piazza. In the gate has a peephole from where he sees outside the home, it seems like the shadow of someone is walking. He does not want to look the shadow so that M turns in the room and picks a book for reading. He does not give attention to the book cover just pick it for changing the state. M's cognisance perpetually penetrates the gloom of such a path where symbolical alchemy. As he reads, the psychology of mind runs on thinking power. 'A sexual demon follows a man and his lust for cutting the organs of sex. A nude demon affectionates in the dreams to a man also.' M stops to read and keep on the table. He perches on the mattress and lays in the straight position. Folded arms put under the head paste chips on the eyelids at the three clocks. As he tries to sleep, he hears stones rattling down across the roof. He unlocks his kernels and swallows the bitter bastard. Precipitate a sound of 'Tomorrow' snoring in his eardrums, and he falls asleep profoundly. The alarm sounds at five accelerate the perception at five clocks. He twists his hand straight, and he finds a leaf on the bed. M whispers how it is possible to get it here. M leaves the sack and turns to the doors and windows and checks. Doors bolted then how? Now he gets ready to find the riddle of the road. Quickly, He burns the diesel for achieving the goal. Within fifteen minutes he is there, as he crosses that way the dark clouds land horrors man. M, as enters the fast blow, trembles and bike daggers, and clouds thud and falls flash on him. But as he arrives in the middle of the path, the force of the miracle pushes him back. Just for once, he efforts to move left turn, and he gets suffice success. But a jerk throws him far and a flashlight clashes tandem. Then he stands in the dark, eyes tightly shut, teeth clenched and hands clamped over ears. And roars in the murky reticence, he strikes the tandem and succours the attitude. He howls on unveil robustness, Who are you! Who are you! Who are you! He jerks feet and says I will go-ahead. He is acting very stupidly, trying to beat them. Now he wiggers in a hole, wheels push on the commencing point. He raises his eyes and sees above, and thinks' Is there any path by which I can search something new!' Just then comes a vague vibration in the earth, and air, quickly change into the violent quiver. For these reasons, M furls like vapour and hops like deer from that path. He passes that way as a fast train and reaches to the home like a cold ice-cream. M direct transpires in his room and fells on the couch. His eyelids shut the doorway, and he leaves thinking part aside. M never speaks anyone at least till the next day. He awakes next to next day and thinks' Am I dreaming?' What was that? Where was I? He occupies and catches the head with two hands. The crest is rolling and rolling then he knocks up and grabs the walk towards out of the room.

Mother: Where were you, son?

M: Hun.

Mother: What am I asking you?

M: You know I was sleeping.

Mother: No, Where were you last to last day? You were absent full day. I called every one though no one knew.

M: Headache is attaching brutally.

Mother: Take a cup of tea with ginger.

M: Mom, I was not really at home?

Mother: Yes, But what happened? Have you forgotten?

M: Can you tell me the mystery is on the earth?

Mother: Yes. But why you are asking?

M: Nothing. Do invisible powers react for itself?

Mother: Yes, Good and bad. Good gives flourishing output, and bad devastates the dynasty for acquiring authority. There no one can go

M: Have you seen this occult?

Mother: I have not directly seen but listen.

M: What have you overhear?

Mother: I have monitored the sounds in the storm and sometimes in a lonely place. You also notice in the desert area a strange vibrations whirl in the hurricane. A swirl in the circle moves in the spiral form. All acquire in the cyclic blow and desolates in itself. My grandmother returned from the bank, where she went for correction in the document she was alone coming and caught in the middle of the road. A whirlwind spirals about half a meal far away and with thuds towards grandmother. She was unconscious about it. Grandmother gawks what is happening. Smoky dust was rotating till slices of clouds. Grandmother gives aside, though whirl collapses the corner of dirt and passes her.

M: You mean, she did not remain there.

Mother: In the swirling sound, nothing audible. You cannot see well in the dusk. Whirl takes everything whatever comes in the path. Swirl's strolling strength swallows because in the spiral winds have intermittent souls. These forces unsatisfied platform touches and sways from one place to another. until they get, and it influences the earth's everything.

M: Unsatisfied souls, how do all know?

Mother: As my grandmother did not know that day was his last day. Our ancestors told us in swirl has servitude souls circulates, and they take away whoever comes on their way. These souls keep earthbound until their desire does not fulfil. After that period, no one could see her, and no one could find her.

M: Did anyone not try to hunt her? Or Did not find her even a single wearing thing?

Mother: No, She became an apparition. Her last funeral rites did as a dead person so that she did not disturb to the coming generation.

M: Did she?

Mother: Yes, She demands living more life in the family member's dreams. Because she was very ambitious and had desires for doing some choosable in her gest, she had aspirations of wandering countries alone.

M: what did she not complete her education? Or Did she spent her whole life in subjugation?

Mother: She was graduate though she hopes to regular her study. But her marriage against want intimidated her to pause a full stop, or she selects after children. But her husband did not like more educated girls, her life cycles in only cleaning dust others.

M: She was the unsatisfied soul who has wants for enjoying life. Can we see her apparition?

Mother: I do not know, but What do you want to know? Why are you ask? Leave this topic. Have your food and relax for healthy ambience.

M stands and goes into the washroom and shaves his beard. Before his bathing meal for him on the table and mom calls him to hurry up. M returns in outside, and on the table, he is enjoying Punjabi food. Punjabi dishes always stuff with ghee and oil, curd and butter, milk and Lassi. In the morning, Punjabi never take bread and jam, and spices stuffed Paranthas are decorating the kitchen and table. The full mouth has not space and time to talk. Later a cup of cardamom, cloves and fennel digest the heavy shoved abdomen. His lethargy body does not allow him to go even in the bedroom so that he sleeps on the sofa. The profound rest and freshness of cooler relax the mind and physique. The ears have lost listening strength and body unconscious and eyeballs in the dark and nose just breathing. The home has lost in the dim and slow and steady day wins with the rays of the sun. And the light of the beams bring out the dusk, tik-tik of the alarm arise the unconscious frame of the skull. As he rises, his hands and eyelid pounce on the mobile. Social media has become a disease for everyone. M also is in the grip of the black demon social media. His valuable period of development spends a maximum of two hours on the perceiving of unknowledgeable programs. Mother is calling and sometimes yelling on him for getting up from the bed so that he can learn the punctuality and drive job on time. His working period commences at ten o clock. Till he sets, he continuously memorizes a sentence' Hurry up Mom, and I am getting late.' He picks up the clothes and even wears the clothes and combs hair, and assembles the essential things a sentence has learned even by the walls,' Hurry up Mom, and I am getting late.' Somehow he reports on the shop at ten o clock but today is a black day for some employees. Teasing is a day entertainer of the boys, and catching customers from the third floor. Where an employee's sustenance decisions dry cleaned by the owner, and a new fresh piece presents for a customer.

Shortlisted rights cannot save even life in this pandemic. In the pestilence, even a single customer is a bulb who lights the dusk for years. An incidence after an instance opens the lockdown when a customer enters the shop without the mask. M for taking a customer comes down from the third floor. As he notices so, he tries to correct him. But the other employee's cold war attack with blame on him he is cracking the customer with the flow of tides thoughts. M returns to his counter on the third floor when the same customer arrives in his section, and he does not pause his tongue. His tongue twists and blames for the unwearying mask. A discussion takes a form of debate no one is aware.

M: Sir, please wears the mask and use hand sanitizer when you enter the store.

Customer: You just do your work. Your work is showing the brand, none other business. It's my choice whether to wear or not. Nothing would happen, Now, show the brands.

M: No, sir, you have to wear the mask after all we all need safety.

Customer: I am not corona positive, ok.

M: I am not saying so.

Customer: Are you corona positive? You utilise the mask.

M: I am not corona positive. Mask uses for safety. It is a refugee helper. Maybe a woman who is with you a corona positive. I do not want to debate. It's a rule of our shop or the government's instruction.

Customer: I will not wear the mask, do whatever you can do.

M: We have not right to display material unless a customer follows our store's guidance.

Customer: I will go to another showroom if you force me.

M: You can go, or It's your desire.

And a customer responds foot from the shop, and M sits aside.

His companion suggests him," You should not react so because he will complain to the owner." M replies to him," He does not bother because we are here thirty members, and all are in risk."

Companion: Manager should aware because the customers arrive on the ground floor first. But he does not do so.

Under the invented light they are sharing their views just then a customer subscribes his shop for shopping. He has a cough and cold, yet he has the mask though he does not wear. The cover has begun a showpiece of the neck of everyone. He demands branded material while he is coughing on the few steps. Marketing boys are looking at each other. And waiting to pause him by a manager, yet he does not so. Others boys maintain a distance for self-security. The customer buys about twenty thousand materials and a manager he shows limitless euphoria before others. Others are under stress for catching in death. That day walks like a trolly. A trolly's whispering sound betokens the wrong coming. The day has resulted out in the veil of others' mind frame. Night's brainstorming alarms early and their fear transform into reality. The owner ahead news before all that a manager has in quarantine, and so no one tries to go his home. The owner commands a guardian and instructs him for checking. Even the heyday's commencing no one acknowledges of unrolling instructions in which a production of starvation runs on the high level. A manager's twenty-one primes for quarantine are tranquillity in the ocean. The store has contracted with varies brands so that the marketer boys are responsible for other companies. In a lockdown, companies are out of the markets, and the market has encompassed with a flood of supply. The companies are showing the inadequacy to paying salaries. The companies are on the intimidation to close the firms due to clamour of demand. Two boys are fire from work in the evening. Fortuitous firing in search of a profession in the Lockdown is a challenge to like the enemy country.

The owner pays sympathy to them and says," Do not worry. I will try to retain you in my store. Although the salary cannot give like company Ok You come tomorrow."

Marketing boys are in trouble for coming threat of unemployment. M in hurriedly calls to other store room's marketing boys and inquire about the condition of companies. He also analyses the changing norms of varies companies and also keeps an eye on the other jobs. He explains the situation of the corporations about work and salaries at home. His father ignores him because he just wants to free service. He lives a life of migrants and wild burden. The family has spoiled before his ego. Next day, two unemployed boys come in the store for meeting to the shop owner, and proprietor suggests them taking for five thousand per month salary. But they refuge to him by saying that it does not suffice for family. M's psychological framework is wheeling under fear and stress. Time has not to limit of giving pressure while the young fearful community get information of deducting fifty per cent salary. As he harks, M's head feels dizziness. The black lights spread the darkness among the boys. After reaching the home, he calls to the manager of the company for paying the full salary. Manager clears all points of the present market with modesty. Forty-five minutes talk does not result out any solution. M's face synchronizes for crying though seeing mother he pauses and sits on the floor lonely.